The Teachers'
Book of Wisdom

The Teachers'
Book of Wisdom

A Celebration of the Joys of Teaching

Compiled and Edited by Criswell Freeman

WALNUT GROVE PRESS
Nashville, TN 37205

ISBN 1-887655-80-8

The ideas expressed in this book are not, in all cases, exact quotations, as some have been edited for clarity and brevity. In all cases, the author has attempted to maintain the speaker's original intent. In some cases, material for this book was obtained from secondary sources, primarily print media. While every effort was made to ensure the accuracy of these sources, the accuracy cannot be guaranteed. For additions, deletions, corrections or clarifications in future editions of this text, please write WALNUT GROVE PRESS.

Printed in the United States of America
Typesetting & Page Layout by Sue Gerdes
Editor for Walnut Grove Press: Alan Ross
3 4 5 6 7 8 9 10 •   99 00 01 02

ACKNOWLEDGMENTS
The author gratefully acknowledges the helpful support of Angela Freeman, Dick and Mary Freeman, and Mary Susan Freeman.
Cover Design by Bart Dawson.

For Donna

Table of Contents

Introduction

Teachers touch the lives of their students on countless occasions. Each time a single life is touched, even in some small way, eternity is re-fashioned.

Teachers change the ways in which their students look at the world. They provide essential tools for life beyond the classroom. What is more important than this?

The quotations in this book celebrate the joys of teaching. May we all continue to teach — and learn — forever.

1

The Joy of Teaching

Molding the minds of young people is a profound responsibility and, at times, a royal headache. Often times, teachers are overburdened with too much work and too little time in which to do it. Despite the inevitable nuisances of grading, preparation, paperwork and classroom discipline, teaching is, at its best, a joyful profession. In this chapter, we consider the delights and responsibilities of the teacher's life.

A teacher affects eternity;
he can never tell where
his influence stops.

Henry Adams

Teaching means helping the child
            realize his potential.

Erich Fromm

It is enough that I am of value to somebody
            today.

Hugh Prather

The entire sum of existence is the magic
      of being needed by just one person.

Vi Putnam

"You are happy," the true ethics whisper.
"Therefore you are called upon to give much."

Albert Schweitzer

Occasionally in life there are moments of
unutterable fulfillment which cannot be
completely explained by those symbols called
words. Their meanings can only be articulated
by the inaudible language of the heart.

Martin Luther King, Jr.

My heart is singing for joy this morning.
A miracle has happened! The light of
understanding has shone upon my little pupil's
mind, and, behold, all things are changed!

Annie Sullivan, Helen Keller's teacher

Teachers not only create a desire for thought,
they give a student experience in thinking.

John Sloan Dickey

All my pupils are the crème de la crème.
Give me a girl of an impressionable age,
and she is mine for life.

Muriel Spark

What office is there which involves more responsibility, which requires more qualifications, and which ought, therefore, to be more honorable than that of teaching?

Harriet Martineau

Every production of genius must be
the production of enthusiasm.

Benjamin Disraeli

A man can succeed at almost anything
for which he has unlimited enthusiasm.

Charles M. Schwab

Man never rises to great truths
without enthusiasm.

Vauvenargues

When enthusiasm is inspired by reason;
controlled by caution; sound in theory;
practical in application; reflects confidence;
spreads good cheer; raises morale; inspires
associates; arouses loyalty; and laughs at
adversity, it is beyond price.

Coleman Cox

People who never get carried away should be.

Malcolm Forbes

Knowledge is power, but enthusiasm
pulls the switch.

Ivern Ball

You will do foolish things, but do them
with enthusiasm.

Colette

Zeal will do more than knowledge.

William Hazlitt

I'm never going to be a movie star. But then, in all probability, Liz Taylor is never going to teach first and second grade.

Mary J. Wilson

The truth is that I am enslaved…in one vast love affair with 70 children.

Sylvia Ashton-Warner

Child, give me your hand that I may walk
    in the light of your faith in me.

Hannah Kahn

To teach is to learn twice.

Joseph Joubert

A teacher makes two ideas
    where only one grew before.

Elbert Hubbard

2

Education Is...

What is education? Education defies simple definition because it occurs in so many different locations and on so many different levels. Of course, education takes place inside the classroom, but it also takes place in countless other settings. We learn from books, teachers, parents, coaches, bosses, and peers. Sometimes, wisdom comes from observation, other times only from bitter experience.

Perhaps the best definition of education was proposed by American philanthropist George Peabody. He said, "Education is a debt from present to future generations." In this chapter, we consider the implications of that debt along with intelligent plans for repayment.

The educated differ from the uneducated as much as the living from the dead.

Aristotle

Education is a chest of tools.

Herbert Kaufman

There are two educations.
One should teach us how to make a living
and the other *how* to live.

James Truslow Adams

Education is hanging on until you've caught on.

Robert Frost

Training is everything. The peach was once a
bitter almond; cauliflower is nothing but cabbage
with a college education.

Mark Twain

The acquisition of knowledge is the mission of research; the transmission of knowledge is the mission of teaching; and the application of knowledge is the mission of public service.

James A. Perkins

Education is a better safeguard of liberty than a standing army.

Edward Everett

Without education, what is man? A splendid slave, a reasoning savage.

Joseph Addison

Only the educated are free.

Epictetus

Education is training for duty.

Berthold Auerbach

Education, beyond all other devices of human origin, is the great equalizer of the conditions of men — the balance-wheel of the social machinery.

Horace Mann

We must see that every child has equal opportunity, not to become equal, but to become different — to realize the unique potential he or she possesses.

John Fischer

Education is that which leads one to the right loves and hatreds.

Lin Yutang

The object of education is to get experience
out of ideas.

George Santayana

The purpose of education is to awaken joy
in creative expression and knowledge.

Albert Einstein

Education: That which discloses to the wise
and disguises from the foolish
their lack of understanding.

Ambrose Bierce

Education is learning
what you didn't know
you didn't know.

Daniel J. Boorstin

Education takes place
in the combination of the
home, the community,
the school, and
the receptive mind.

Harry Edwards

Not the school,
nor the teachers,
but the student is the
preponderant factor
in education.

James Weldon Johnson

A degree is not an education,
and the confusion on this point is perhaps
the gravest weakness in education.

Rockefeller Brothers Fund

Much that passes for education is not
education at all, but ritual. The fact is that we
are being educated when we know it least.

David P. Gardner

To be able to be caught up into the world
of thought — that is education.

Edith Hamilton

An education isn't how much you have
committed to memory. It's knowing where to
go to find out what you need to know, and it's
knowing how to use the information you get.

William Feather

Education means capacity
for further education.

John Dewey

Knowledge is not simply
another commodity.
To the contrary,
knowledge is never used up.
It increases by diffusion
and grows by dispersion.

Daniel J. Boorstin

Education should
convert the mind into
a living fountain
and not a reservoir.

John M. Mason

There are few earthly things more beautiful
than a university.

John Masefield

Universities should be safe havens where
ruthless examination of realities will not be
distorted by the aim to please or inhibited
by the risk of displeasure.

Kingman Brewster

A university's essential character is that of
being a center of free inquiry and criticism —
a thing not to be sacrificed for anything else.

Richard Hofstadter

College is a refuge from hasty judgment.

Robert Frost

The most important function of education
at any level is to develop the personality of the
individual and the significance of his life
to himself and to others.

Grayson Kirk

The teacher's task is not to implant facts
but to place the subject to be learned in front
of the learner and, through sympathy, emotion,
imagination and patience, to awaken in the
learner the restless drive for answers and
insights which enlarge the personal life
and give it meaning.

Nathan M. Pusey

Via ovicipitum dura est.
The way of the egghead is hard.

Adlai E. Stevenson

Education is a kind of continuing dialogue,
and a dialogue assumes different points of view.

Robert M. Hutchins

Education is the ability to listen to almost
anything without losing your temper
or your self-confidence.

Robert Frost

Education is a matter of building bridges.

Ralph Ellison

The ability to think straight, some knowledge
of the past, some vision of the future, some skill
to do useful service, some urge to fit that
service into the well-being of the community —
these are the most vital things education
must try to produce.

Virginia Gildersleeve

Real education should educate us out of self
into something far finer — into selflessness
which links us with all humanity.

Nancy Astor

Real education consists in drawing the best
out of yourself. What better book can there be
than the book of humanity.

Mohandas Gandhi

The basic purpose of a liberal arts education
is to liberate the human being to exercise
his or her potential to the fullest.

Barbara M. White

Education is the seeing of things in the working.

Thomas Alva Edison

Education is what
survives when what
has been learned
has been forgotten.

B. F. Skinner

If you think education is expensive, try ignorance.

Derek Bok

3

The Power of Education

Francis Bacon wrote, "Knowledge and human power are synonymous." His words are truer today than ever. By and large, the uneducated must play the entire game of life on an uneven field. But the value of education is often invisible to young people who rebel against the very tool that might level the field on which they play — or even tilt it in their direction.

Fairness and common sense dictate that every boy and girl be given a meaningful opportunity to learn; the rest, of course, is out of teachers' hands. Only parents and students possess the ability to harness the power of education, but good teachers can show them how.

If there is anything in the world that can really be called a man's property, it is surely that which is the result of his mental activity.

Arthur Schopenhauer

Better to have education than wealth.

Welsh Proverb

If we work upon marble, it will perish; if we work on brass, time will efface it. If we rear temples, they will crumble to dust. But if we work on men's immortal minds, if we impress on them high principles, the just fear of God, and love for their fellowmen, we engrave on those tablets something which no time can efface and which will brighten and brighten to all eternity.

Daniel Webster

The aim of education is the knowledge not of facts but of values.

William Ralph Inge

He knows enough who knows how to learn.

Henry Adams

Perhaps the most valuable result of education
is the ability to make yourself do the thing you
have to do, when it ought to be done, whether
you like it or not.

Walter Bagehot

The test and the use of man's education
is that he finds pleasure in the exercise
of his mind.

Jacques Barzun

Learning makes a man fit company
for himself.

Thomas Fuller

Think wrongly, if you please, but in all cases, think for yourself.

Doris Lessing

The efficient man is the man who thinks for himself.

Charles W. Eliot

Curiosity is the one permanent and certain characteristic of a vigorous mind.

Samuel Johnson

Intelligence is quickness in seeing things as they are.

George Santayana

The human mind is our fundamental resource.

John F. Kennedy

In the realm of ideas, it is better to let the mind sally forth, even if some precious preconceptions suffer a mauling.

Robert F. Goheen

Any education that matters is liberal. All the saving truths, all the healing graces that distinguish a good education from a bad one or a full education from a half empty one are contained in that word.

Alan Simpson

An educated man is one who can entertain a new idea, entertain another person, and entertain himself.

Sydney Wood

An educated man thinks for himself.

Alan Simpson

There is no influence so powerful as that
of the mother, but next in rank of efficacy
is that of the schoolmaster.

Sarah Josepha Hale

If you drop out, you miss out.

Bill Cosby

The mind's cross-indexing puts the best
librarian to shame.

Sharon Begley

Genius means little more than the faculty
of perceiving in an unhabitual way.

William James

Whether you think you can or think you can't,
you're right.

Henry Ford

The direction of the mind
is more important
than its progress.

Joseph Joubert

The benefits of education and of useful knowledge, generally diffused through a community, are essential to the preservation of a free government.

Sam Houston

Nothing can possibly afford greater stability to a popular government than the education of its people.

Samuel Whitbread

Upon the education of the people of this country the fate of this country depends.

Benjamin Disraeli

Education is the foundation of governance.

Jacob H. Carruthers

I know no safe depository of the ultimate powers of the society but the people themselves; and if we think them not enlightened enough to exercise their control with a wholesome discretion, the remedy is not to take it from them but to inform their discretion by education. This is the true corrective of abuses of constitutional power.

Thomas Jefferson

Enlighten the people generally, and tyranny and oppressions of body and mind will vanish like evil spirits at the dawn of day.

Thomas Jefferson

It is safer to have a whole people respectably enlightened than a few in a high state of science and the many in ignorance.

Thomas Jefferson

In the long course of history, having an educated electorate is much greater security than another submarine.

J. William Fulbright

Just as those who have to live upon coarse
food may show its effects in their body, so
those whose minds are fed upon pure thought,
whether of Longfellow or Whittier or any
other first-class poet, will soon show in their
spiritual development what they have
been studying.

Fanny Jackson Coppin

To educate a man in mind and not in morals
is to educate a menace to society.

Theodore Roosevelt

Education has for its object the formation
of character. This is the aim of both
parent and teacher.

Herbert Spencer

Human history becomes
more and more a race
between education
and catastrophe.

H. G. Wells

Give a man a fish and
you feed him for a day.
Teach a man to fish
and you feed him
for a lifetime.

Chinese   Proverb

4

The Learning Experience

Aristotle observed, "All men by nature desire to learn." It might be added that some men seem to desire it more than others. And what makes the difference? In part, the difference is superior teaching. Outstanding teachers do much more than convey knowledge; they also spur the desire to learn.

British mathematician Alfred North Whitehead wrote, "From the very beginning of his education, the child should experience the joy of discovery." The learning experience is, at its best, a grand adventure with teachers serving as tour guides. The following ideas will help in planning the tour.

Only the curious will learn, and only the resolute will overcome the obstacles to learning. The quest quotient has always excited me more than the intelligence quotient.

Eugene S. Wilson

No one ever became wise by chance.

Seneca

Learning is a natural pleasure, inborn and instinctive, one of the earliest pleasures and one of the essential pleasures of the human race.

Gilbert Highet

Learning is the discovery that something is possible.

Fritz Perls

Some people never learn
anything because they
understand everything
too soon.

Alexander Pope

To live for a time close to great minds
is the best kind of education.

John Buchan

We learn simply by the exposure of living,
and what we learn most natively
is the tradition in which we live.

David P. Gardner

Too often, for many of us, learning appears
to be an imposition, a surrender of our own
willpower to external direction, indeed a sort
of enslavement. This is a mistake.

Gilbert Highet

To learn is very pleasant, not only
for philosophers, but for other men too,
except that they enjoy it on a smaller scale.

Aristotle

Learning means keeping the mind open and active to receive all kinds of experience.

Gilbert Highet

The function of education is to teach one to think intensively and to think critically. Intelligence plus character — that is the goal of true education.

Martin Luther King, Jr.

What a teacher doesn't say is a telling part of what a student hears.

Maurice Natanson

The process of learning can and must become
not only one of growing but also of sharing.

Joe Nathan

All learning proceeds by steps. Absences of
pupils are like a ladder with a rung out here
and there. Instead of going up easily,
the student every now and then is distracted
by the difficulty of the step.

Fanny Jackson Coppin

Learning is more difficult for the young
if it is a "have-to" imposed by authority.

Gilbert Highet

All our children deserve teachers
      who believe they can learn and who
      will not be satisfied until they do.

Joe Nathan

Learning cannot be inherited.

Yiddish Proverb

If they are willing to learn, the quality
      of their lives will improve.

William Glasser, M.D.

Even if we live for ninety years, we can never
exhaust the pleasures of poetry or art or music.

Gilbert Highet

I was still learning when I taught my last class.

Claude M. Fuess

The purpose of education is the discipline of mind for its own sake.

Allen Tate

Most of the important experiences
that truly educate cannot be arranged
ahead of time with any precision.

Harold Taylor

Schoolmasters and parents exist
to be grown out of.

John Wolfenden

Four years was enough of Harvard. I still had
a lot to learn but had been given the liberating
notion that now I could teach myself.

John Updike

Could *Hamlet* have been written by a
committee, or the Mona Lisa painted by a club?
Could the New Testament have been composed
as a conference report? Creative ideas do not
spring from groups. They spring from
individuals. The divine spark leaps from
the finger of God to the finger of Adam.

A. Whitney Griswold

When the pupil is ready, the teacher will come.

Chinese Saying

5

Books

Noted psychologist B. F. Skinner observed, "We shouldn't teach great books; we should teach a love of reading." The ability to enjoy a good book is an acquired skill that pays lifelong dividends. The following quotations celebrate the joy of reading. Let the celebration begin!

To acquire the habit
of reading is to construct
for yourself a refuge from
almost all the miseries
of life.

Somerset Maugham

There is more treasure in books than in all the pirate's loot on Treasure Island.

Walt Disney

Books are a guide in youth
and an entertainment in old age.

Jeremy Collier

Books are the very heart and core
of ages past.

Amy Lowell

A good book is opened with expectation
and closed with profit.

Bronson Alcott

A book is a garden carried in the pocket.

Arabian Proverb

Books are friends
that never fail.

Thomas Carlyle

Books are the windows through which
the souls look out.

Henry Ward Beecher

Books are not made for furniture,
but there is nothing else that so beautifully
furnishes a house.

Henry Ward Beecher

Books are the true university.

Thomas Carlyle

The best effect of any book is that it excites the reader to self-activity.

Thomas Carlyle

Happy are the children whose parents know the importance of teaching them to love and care for books while they are young.

Fanny Jackson Coppin

A good library is a joyful place
　　where the imagination roams free,
　　and life is actively enriched.

John K. Hutchens

A library, to modify the famous metaphor
of Socrates, should be the delivery room for
the birth of ideas — a place where history
comes to life.

Norman Cousins

Libraries keep the records
　　on behalf of all humanity.

Vartan Gregorian

Reading books contains two different delights, both definable as learning. One is the pleasure of apprehending the unexpected: when one meets a new author who has a new vision of the world. The other is the pleasure of deepening one's knowledge of a special field.

Gilbert Highet

The very concept of history implies the scholar and the reader. Without a generation of civilized people to study history, to preserve its records, to absorb its lessons and relate them to its own problems, history, too, would lose its meaning.

George F. Kennan

The elementary school must assume as its sublime and most solemn responsibility the task of teaching every child in it to read. Any school that does not accomplish this has failed.

Jacques Barzun

Sometimes when I stand in a big library,
I feel a sober, earnest delight which is hard to
convey. These are not books, lumps of lifeless
paper, but *minds* alive on the shelves.

Gilbert Highet

There are times when I think that the ideal
library is composed solely of reference books.
They are like understanding friends — always
ready to meet your mood, always ready to
change the subject when you have had
enough of this or that.

J. Donald Adams

What is important — what lasts — in another
language is not what is said but what is written.
For the essence of an age, we look to its poetry
and its prose, not its talk shows.

Peter Brodie

Books are the fit inheritance of generations and nations.

Henry David Thoreau

6

The Art of Teaching

Exceptional teachers come in many shapes and sizes, but they all share a few essential traits. The best instructors not only challenge their students but also encourage them. Outstanding teachers also entertain while they educate. Finally, exceptional teachers understand that the most important lesson — and the teacher's greatest challenge — is to instill the love of learning in the heart of the pupil.

Great educators, like great artists, create works that outlive their creators. Teachers leave their mark on a human canvas. In this chapter, we consider ways to improve the artwork.

 A teacher who is attempting to teach
without inspiring the pupil with a desire to learn
is hammering on cold iron.

Horace Mann

 What is really important in education is not
that the child learn this and that, but that the
mind is matured and energy is aroused.

Søren Kierkegaard

 Teaching is the art of assisting discovery.

Mark Van Doren

 Teaching is the art of appearing to have known
all your life what you learned this afternoon.

Anonymous

When you are dealing with a child, keep your wits about you and sit on the floor.

Austin O'Malley

Better than a thousand days of diligent study
is one day with a great teacher.

Japanese Proverb

A great teacher makes hard things easy.

Ralph Waldo Emerson

A good teacher, like a good entertainer,
first must hold his audience's attention.
Then he can teach the lesson.

John Henrik Clarke

The greatest artist is the simplifier.

Henri Frédéric Amiel

A teacher is one who brings us tools
and enables us to use them.

Jean Toomer

Teaching is an instinctual art, mindful of potential, craving of realization, a pausing, seamless process.

A. Bartlett Giamatti

You never replace a great scholar who retires. If you try to do that, you end up with burnt-out volcanoes.

Guido Calabresi

Teaching is not a lost art, but the regard for it is a lost tradition.

Jacques Barzun

Human beings are full of emotion, and the teacher who knows how to use it will have dedicated learners.

Leon Lessinger

Teachers believe they have a gift for giving;
it drives them with the same irrepressible drive
that drives others to create a work of art or
a market or a building.

A. Bartlett Giamatti

The art of teaching is the art of awakening
the natural curiosity of young minds.

Anatole France

On a good day, I view the job as directing
an orchestra. On the dark days, it is more like
that of a clutch — engaging the engine
to effect forward motion.

A. Bartlett Giamatti

A teacher must believe in the value and
interest of his subject as a doctor believes
in health.

Gilbert Highet

Effective teaching will not always be entertaining, but it will engage youngsters in thoughtful, productive activity.

Joe Nathan

I have one rule — attention. They give me theirs, and I give them mine.

Sister Evangelist RSM

The good teacher discovers the natural gifts of his pupils and liberates them by the stimulating influence of the inspiration that he can impart. The true leader makes his followers twice the men they were before.

Stephen Neill

A substantial body of research supports the common-sense notion that young people do not learn as much in a threatening environment as in a supportive one.

Joe Nathan

The only gift is a portion of thyself.
Ralph Waldo Emerson

Be kind, for everyone you meet is fighting
a hard battle.
Plato

The only reason I always try to meet and
know the parents better is because it
helps me to forgive their children.
Louis Johannot

Everyone knows a good deal
about one child — himself.
Dora Chaplin

Who dares to teach must never cease to learn.

John Cotton Dana

Men learn while they teach.

Seneca

Above all, leave room for your own learning — for the chance to discover and teach something you didn't know when the course began.

Wayne C. Booth

Every class should be for you as much as for the students.

Wayne C. Booth

As you teach, emphasize what interests you.

William Glasser, M.D.

All teachers know enough to know that only useful work can provide the incentive students need to expend the effort to do quality work.

William Glasser, M.D.

If we think about our own lives, we'll remember how much more we learned from those who encouraged us.

Joe Nathan

Teaching demands not just desirable personality attributes but specific skills. Skills are not ends in themselves, but they are necessary tools.

Jacob S. Kounin

Many a child called dull would advance rapidly under a patient, wise and skillful teacher, and the teacher should be as conscientious in the endeavor to improve himself as he is to improve the child.

Fanny Jackson Coppin

A liberal education is at the heart of a civil society, and at the heart of a liberal education is the act of teaching.

A. Bartlett Giamatti

Teachers must think for themselves if they are to help others think for themselves.

Carnegie Corporation of New York

I had learned to respect the intelligence, integrity, creativity and capacity for deep thought and hard work latent somewhere in every child.

Sybil Marshall

A teacher is the child's third parent.

Hyman Maxwell Berston

7

The Student

Turn-of-the-century educator Fanny Jackson Coppin noted, "I'm always sorry to hear that a person is going to school to be educated. This is a great mistake. If a person is to get the benefit of what we call education, he must educate himself, under the direction of the teacher." In other words, you can lead a boy to wonder, but you can't make him think.

The following quotations give insight into the hearts and minds of those who, in the end, must educate themselves. And when they do, it's wonderful.

Happy is the child who has wise parents
and guardians and whose training is
continued when he enters the school room.

Fanny Jackson Coppin

I see the mind of the 5-year-old
as a volcano with two vents:
destructiveness and creativeness.

Sylvia Ashton-Warner

The teacher can lead a student to the door;
the acquisition of learning is the
responsibility of the student.

Chinese Proverb

All students can learn.

Christopher Morley

A child miseducated
is a child lost.

John F. Kennedy

Most of the trouble and friction among people,
in or out of school, is caused
by putting others down.

William Glasser, M.D.

A child must feel the flush of victory and the
heart-sinking of disappointment before he takes
with a will to the tasks distasteful to him
and resolves to dance his way through
a dull routine of textbooks.

Helen Keller

Start a program for gifted children, and every
parent demands that his child be enrolled.

Thomas Bailey

There must be such a thing as a child with
average ability, but you can't find a parent
who will admit that it is his child.

Thomas Bailey

A student is not a professional athlete.
He is not a little politician or junior senator
looking for angles. A student is a person who
is learning to fulfill his powers and to find
ways of using them in the service of mankind.

Harold Taylor

Young people need to feel that their ideas
and skills are valued.

Joe Nathan

Anyone who's watched a school's doors
at the end of the day knows how much human
energy bursts out at the final bell. The
potential is there, waiting to be stimulated,
challenged, and encouraged.

Joe Nathan

If you promise not to believe everything your
child says happens at this school, I'll promise
not to believe everything he says happens
at home.

Anonymous English Schoolmaster

We cannot learn from one another until
we stop shouting at one another, until we speak
quietly enough so that our words can be heard
as well as our voices.

Richard M. Nixon

Work 'em hard, play 'em hard, feed 'em up to
the nines and send 'em to bed so tired that they
are asleep before their heads are on the pillow.

Frank L. Boyden

Students welcome any change from routine.

William Glasser, M.D.

The quality of a university is measured more
by the kind of student it turns out than the kind
it takes in.

Robert J. Kibbee

In the conditions of modern life, the rule
is absolute: Those who do not value trained
intelligence are doomed. There is no appeal
from the judgment which is pronounced
on the uneducated.

Alfred North Whitehead

Let early education be
a sort of amusement;
you will then be better
able to discover the
child's natural bent.

Plato

If you plan for a year, plant a seed. If for ten years, plant a tree. If for a hundred years, teach the people. When you sow a seed once, you will reap a single harvest. When you teach the people, you will reap a hundred harvests.

Kuan Chung

8

Homework

When times get tough in the old school-house, most students react in a similar fashion: They blame the teacher. This blame is almost always misdirected. Pupils are advised to contemplate the words of Shakespeare's Cassius, who admitted, "The fault, dear Brutus, is not in our stars, but in ourselves…"

Socrates observed, "If a man would move the world, he must first move himself." And so it is with education. The student who wishes to move to the head of the class must begin by moving himself in that direction. While the teacher may help show the way, the student himself makes the journey. If the results of that journey are unsatisfactory, it profits no one to accuse instructors, institutions, or the heavens. Any pupil who feels the urge to blame a teacher should try a more constructive strategy: doing the homework.

The day is short, the labor long,
the workers are idle, the reward is great,
and the Master is urgent.

Rabbi Tarfon

Being ignorant is not so much a shame
as being unwilling to learn.

Ben Franklin

The main value of homework lies in the
experience it gives a child to work on his own.

Haim Ginott

When you have a number of disagreeable
duties to perform, always do the most
disagreeable first.

Josiah Quincy

The world belongs to the energetic.

Ralph Waldo Emerson

Well done is better than well said.

Ben Franklin

I do not know anyone who has got to the top
without hard work. That's the recipe.
It will not always get you to the top
but should get you pretty near.

Margaret Thatcher

The reward of a thing well done
is to have done it.

Ralph Waldo Emerson

Perseverance can do anything
   which genius can do and very many things
            which genius cannot.

Henry Ward Beecher

It is not labor that kills but the small
   attritions of daily routine that wear us down.

Roy Bedicheck

Our greatest weariness comes
            from work not done.

Eric Hoffer

There is nothing so fatal to character
            as half-finished tasks.

David Lloyd George

Fear is nature's warning
sign to get busy.

Henry C. Link

Work is not a curse.
It is the prerogative
of the intelligent.

Calvin Coolidge

It is work, work that one delights in, that is
the surest guarantor of happiness. But even
here it is a work that has to be earned by
labor in one's earlier years. One should labor
so hard in youth that everything one does
subsequently is easy by comparison.

Ashley Montagu

The more I want to get something done,
the less I call it work.

Richard Bach

The notion that work is a burden is a terrible
mistake. Working and facing up to one's
responsibilities: That's happiness.

Katharine Hepburn

There is no shame in asking for help.

William Glasser, M.D.

The only way to teach them to write correctly
is to have them write. A good rule would be to
have pupils write a little essay once a week.

Fanny Jackson Coppin

Life is easier when parents deliberately ignore
the daily details of their child's homework.
School assignments are the responsibility
of the child. As one father said to his son,
"Homework is for you what work is for me —
a personal responsibility."

Haim Ginott

We teachers can only help the work going on,
as servants wait upon a master.

Maria Montessori

9

Order in the Classroom

The noted writer E. B. White once observed, "If you make the work interesting, the discipline will take care of itself." Obviously, Mr. White never taught junior high. If classroom discipline were solely dependent upon subject matter, teachers everywhere could quiet their students with a few verses from Shakespeare. Unfortunately, it's not that easy.

A more realistic assessment of schoolhouse comportment was offered by Haim Ginott, who wrote, "Every teacher knows that 'Love is not enough.' Neither is 'Creating rapport' or 'Making it interesting.' Friendly adjectives do not a classroom problem solve."

The ideas contained in this chapter will not resolve all classroom difficulties, but they will help. And, if all else fails, try Shakespeare.

Education is teaching children to behave
as they prefer not to behave.

Anonymous

To expect to rule others by assuming a loud
tone is like thinking oneself tall by putting
on high heels.

J. Petit-Senn

The inner landscape of many children is full of
mines ready to explode upon careless contact.
Any insulting remark can set off an explosion.

Haim Ginott

Whenever a pupil has spoken disrespectfully
to a teacher and the teacher can say with truth,
"Do I not always speak politely to you?"
the case is won without any more argument.

Fanny Jackson Coppin

In discipline, whatever generates hate
must be avoided. Whatever creates self-esteem
is to be fostered.

Haim Ginott

Good discipline is a series of little victories in which a teacher, through small decencies, reaches a child's heart.

Haim Ginott

Disciplinary problems become opportunities
for conveying values, providing insights,
and strengthening self-esteem.

Haim Ginott

I never reprimand a boy in the evening —
darkness and a troubled mind
are a poor combination.

Frank L. Boyden

When a child feels he does not deserve praise,
he may misbehave to set the adult straight.

Haim Ginott

Discipline, like surgery, requires precision —
no random cuts, no rambling comments.
Above all, a teacher demonstrates
self-discipline and good manners.

Haim Ginott

I can think of no agency in the formation of a beautiful character that is more powerful than the daily correction and training which we call discipline, and here the teacher is all-powerful.

Fanny Jackson Coppin

Discipline of the school should proceed from the life of the school as a whole and not directly from the teacher.

John Dewey

Living up to basic ethical standards in the classroom — discipline, tolerance, honesty — is one of the most important ways children learn how to function in society at large.

Eloise Salholz

Your job is to teach students that their behavior is not caused by what happened to them, but by what goes on inside their heads; and that whatever they do, they are choosing to do it.

William Glasser, M.D.

Talking in classes disturbs the teacher and the class. The habit of self-control is not easily acquired, but when the pupil has his tongue under control, as St. James says, "He is able also to bridle the whole body."

Fanny Jackson Coppin

Calming down a noisy, rebellious group of adolescents is a lot like defusing a bomb. Careful, premeditated, calm responses are crucial to success.

James Nehring

Self-control is the highest form of rulership.
Apocrypha

Self-control is the hardest victory.
Aristotle

Self-control is the ability to restrain a laugh
at the wrong place.
Elbert Hubbard

Punishments that do not correct, harden.
Fanny Jackson Coppin

Every misbehaving child is discouraged and
needs continuous encouragement, just as
a plant needs water and sunshine.
Rudolf Dreikurs

I have thought about it a great deal, and the more I think, the more certain I am that obedience is the gateway through which knowledge, yes, and love, too, enter the mind of the child.

Annie Sullivan

Keep cool; anger is not an argument.

Daniel Webster

10

Lessons About Life

W. E. B. Du Bois observed, "Education must not simply teach work, it must teach life." In this chapter, we consider a few of the most important lessons about the human condition.

Life is a series of lessons
that must be lived
to be understood.

Ralph Waldo Emerson

May everything I see teach and instruct me something.

Margaret Godolphin

Education is life, not books.

African Proverb

What education I have received has been gained in the University of Life.

Horatio Bottomley

Life is painting a picture, not doing a sum.

Oliver Wendell Holmes, Jr.

Be yourself and think for yourself; and, while your conclusions may not be infallible, they will be nearer right than the conclusions forced upon you.

Elbert Hubbard

Great minds have purposes;
      others have wishes.

Washington Irving

Believe that your life is worth living,
      and your belief will help create the fact.

William James

Every man's life is a plan of God.

Horace Bushnell

Every man is the architect of his own fortune.

Sallust

Life is the sum of all your choices.

Albert Camus

A human life is like a single letter in the alphabet. It can be meaningless. Or it can be part of a great meaning.

Jewish Theological Seminary of America

Life is a fatal adventure. It can only have one end. So why not make it as far-ranging and free as possible?

Alexander Eliot

Life is a great bundle of little things.

Oliver Wendell Holmes, Sr.

Life is a succession of moments; to live each one is to succeed.

Corita Kent

All life is an experiment. The more experiments you make, the better.

Ralph Waldo Emerson

Opportunity is missed by most people
because it is dressed in overalls
and looks like work.

Thomas Alva Edison

Life is always at some turning point.

Irwin Edman

There is no security on this earth;
there is only opportunity.

Douglas MacArthur

When fate hands you a lemon,
make lemonade.

Dale Carnegie

To improve the golden moment of opportunity
and catch the good that is within our reach
is the great art of life.

Samuel Johnson

The world is all gates,
all opportunities, strings
of tension waiting
to be struck.

Ralph Waldo Emerson

The aim of a college education is to teach you to know a good man when you see one.

William James

Words, words, how they can make or mar our lives!

Fanny Jackson Coppin

To learn to give up his own will to that of his parents or teacher, as we must to the Great Teacher of all, will surely make us happy in this life and in the life to come.

Fanny Jackson Coppin

11

The School of Hard Knocks

Frederick Phillips noted, "It is often hard to distinguish between the hard knocks in life and those of opportunity." Anyone who has been knocked down by life will attest that these opportunities are not only hard to see but sometimes are almost invisible.

American poet Ella Wheeler Wilcox wrote, "From the discontent of man, the world's best progress springs." In this chapter we consider the entrance requirements, the curriculum, and the honored graduates of a school that has changed the world like no other: the school of hard knocks.

Times of general calamity and confusion
have ever been productive of the greatest
minds. The purest ore is produced from the
hottest furnace, and the brightest thunder-
bolt is elicited from the darkest storms.

Charles Caleb Colton

Problems are the cutting edge that
distinguishes between success and failure.
Problems create our courage and wisdom.

M. Scott Peck

Good people are good because
they've come to wisdom through failure.

William Saroyan

Obstacles cannot crush me; every obstacle
yields to stern resolve.

Leonardo da Vinci

God helps those who persevere.

The Koran

Do you desire to know the art of living my friend? It is contained in one phrase: Make use of suffering.

Henri Frédéric Amiel

A problem is a chance for you
to do your best.

Duke Ellington

The game of life is not so much in holding
a good hand as playing a poor hand well.

H. T. Leslie

No pain, no palm; no thorns, no throne;
no gall, no glory; no cross, no crown.

William Penn

Problems are the price of progress.
Don't bring me anything but trouble.

Charles F. Kettering

Adversity causes some men to break,
others to break records.

William A. Ward

The difficulties and struggles of today are but the price we must pay for the accomplishments and victories of tomorrow.

William J. H. Boetcker

Real miracles are created by men when they use their God-given courage and intelligence.

Jean Anouilh

Of all the advantages which come to any young man, poverty is the greatest.

Josiah G. Holland

Poverty must not be a bar to learning, and learning must offer an escape from poverty.

Lyndon B. Johnson

With luck and resolution and good guidance, the human mind can survive not only poverty — but even wealth.

Gilbert Highet

Adversity introduces a man to himself.

Unknown

Our trials are tests; our sorrows pave the way for a fuller life when we have earned it.

Jerome P. Fleishman

It was darkness which produced the lamp.
It was fog that produced the compass.
And it took a depression to teach us
the real value of a job.

Victor Hugo

The gem cannot be polished without friction
nor man perfected without trials.

Confucius

A diamond is a chunk
of coal that made good
under pressure.

Unknown

People seldom see the halting and painful steps by which the most insignificant success is achieved.

Annie Sullivan

Character cannot be developed in ease and quiet. Only through the experience of trial and suffering can the soul be strengthened, vision cleared, ambition inspired, and success achieved.

Helen Keller

Difficulties are meant to rouse,
    not discourage. The human spirit grows
        strong by conflict.

William Ellery Channing

Chance favors the prepared mind.

Louis Pasteur

He that wrestles with us strengthens our
    nerves and sharpens our skills.
    Our antagonist is our helper.

Edmund Burke

The block of granite which was an obstacle
    in the path of the weak becomes
    a stepping-stone in the path of the strong.

Thomas Carlyle

Although there are countless alumni of the
school of hard knocks, there has not yet been
    a move to accredit that institution.

Sonya Rudikoff

12

Lessons Beyond the Classroom

Every student who has ever suffered through a long-winded graduation speech has heard the same message: Graduation should mark the commencement, not the conclusion of learning. One is reminded of the wise old professor who once remarked, "A college education never hurt anyone willing to learn something afterward." This fact was not lost on philosopher George Santayana, who wrote, "The wisest mind has something yet to learn." Here's how.

Lessons Beyond the Classroom

They go forth with well-developed bodies,
fairly developed minds, and undeveloped hearts.
An undeveloped heart — not a cold one.
The difference is important.

E.M. Forster

The fireworks begin today.
Each diploma is a lighted match.
Each one of you is a fuse.

Edward Koch

I ask you to decide, as Goethe put it,
whether you will be an anvil or a hammer. The
question is whether you are to be a hammer —
whether you are to give to the world in which
you were reared and educated the broadest
possible benefits of that education.

John F. Kennedy

My job is to bore you and let the hardness
of your seat and the warmth of your robe
prepare you for what is to come.

William H. McNeill

It is no profit to have learned well if you neglect to do well.

Publilius Syrus

The secret of joy in work is contained in one
word — excellence. To know how to do
something well is to enjoy it.

Pearl Buck

Always aim for achievement,
and forget about success.

Helen Hayes

The most unhappy of all men is the man
who cannot tell what he is going to do,
who has got no work cut out for him in the
world, and does not go into it. For work is the
grand cure of all the maladies and miseries
that ever beset mankind — honest work,
which you intend getting done.

Thomas Carlyle

In an absorbing vocation, working hours are
never long enough. Each day is a holiday,
and ordinary holidays are grudged
as enforced interruptions.

Sir Winston Churchill

Nothing is really work unless you would
rather be doing something else.

Sir James M. Barrie

I think a poet is a workman. I think
Shakespeare was a workman. And God's
a workman. I don't think there's anything
better than a workman.

Laurence Olivier

The work of the individual still remains
the spark that moves mankind ahead,
even more than teamwork.

Igor Sikorsky

I long to accomplish a great and noble task,
but it is my chief duty to accomplish humble
tasks as though they were great and noble.
The world is moved along, not only by the
mighty shoves of its heroes but also by the
aggregate of the tiny pushes
of each honest worker.

Helen Keller

The most instructive experiences
are those of everyday life.

Friedrich Nietzsche

Time is a great teacher.

Carl Sandburg

Lessons Beyond the Classroom

Observations more than books, experiences rather than persons are the prime educators.

Bronson Alcott

As long as you live, keep learning
how to live.

Seneca

Instruction ends in the schoolroom,
but education ends only with life.

F. W. Robertson

It is always in season for old men to learn.

Aeschylus

It is better to learn late than never.

Publilius Syrus

The essence of knowledge is, having it,
to use it.

Confucius

Anyone who stops learning is old,
whether at twenty or eighty.

Henry Ford

A man, though wise, should never be
ashamed of learning more.

Sophocles

A man should never stop learning,
even on his last day.

Maimonides

One's work may be finished some day,
but one's education, never.

Alexandre Dumas

When you're green, you're growing;
when you're ripe, you rot.

Ray Kroc

It's what you learn after you know it all that counts.

Harry S. Truman

13

Observations About Learning

We conclude with a potpourri of learned thoughts from an assortment of learned sources. Enjoy!

Get your students talking to each other,
not just to you or to the air.

Wayne C. Booth

The doer alone learneth.

Friedrich Nietzsche

Listen rather than lecture.
Show the road but expect the child to reach
his destination on his own.

Haim Ginott

Use fewer examinations, fewer quizzes,
and more essay assignments. You don't know
anything about a subject until you can put
your knowledge into some kind of expression.

Wayne C. Booth

We teach who we are.

John Gardner

We have ignored cultural literacy in thinking
about education. Cultural literacy
is the oxygen of social intercourse.

E. D. Hirsch, Jr.

Good manners will often take people where
neither money nor education will take them.

Fanny Jackson Coppin

Wisdom is oftentimes nearer when we stoop
than when we soar.

William Wordsworth

What we have to learn to do,
we learn by doing.

Aristotle

My definition of an educated man is the
fellow who knows the right thing to do
at the time it has to be done.

Charles F. Kettering

We live in a time of such rapid change
and growth of knowledge that only he who
is in a fundamental sense a scholar — that is,
a person who continues to learn and inquire —
can hope to keep pace, let alone play
the role of guide.

Nathan M. Pusey

The problem is not to suppress change,
which cannot be done, but to manage it.

Alvin Toffler

Only in growth, reform, and change,
paradoxically enough, is true security found.

Anne Morrow Lindbergh

A man must consider what a rich realm
he abdicates when he becomes a conformist.

Ralph Waldo Emerson

Education consists mainly
in what we have unlearned.

Mark Twain

I think we have a need
to know what we do not
need to know.

William Safire

The art of being wise is knowing
what to overlook.

William James

Love wins when everything else will fail.

Fanny Jackson Coppin

Life is a festival only to the wise.

Ralph Waldo Emerson

I am still learning.

Michelangelo's Favorite Saying

I am not young enough to know everything.

Sir James M. Barrie

Unholy ambition never succeeds well in
anything, nor will the Great Creator reveal
His secrets to those whose only desire is
to shine in the eyes of men. But the light of
Heaven will shine all around the man who
humbly and fervently asks for more light,
more light.

Fanny Jackson Coppin

I am quite sure that in the hereafter
my teacher will take me by the hand
and lead me to my proper seat.

Bernard Baruch

What we are is God's gift to us. What we become is our gift to God.

Eleanor Powell

Sources

Sources

Sources

Friedrich Nietzsche 143, 148
Richard M. Nixon 100
Laurence Olivier 143
Austin O'Malley 85
Louis Pasteur 138
George Peabody 25
M. Scott Peck 130
William Penn 132
James A. Perkins 28
Fritz Perls 62
J. Petit-Senn 112
Frederick Phillips 129
Plato 90, 101
Alexander Pope 63
Eleanor Powell 154
Hugh Prather 17
Publilius Syrus 141, 144
Nathan M. Pusey 39, 150
Vi Putnam 17
Josiah Quincy 104
F. W. Robertson 144
Theodore Roosevelt 58
Sonya Rudikoff 138
William Safire 151
Eloise Salholz 117
Sallust 124
Carl Sandburg 143
George Santayana 30, 50
William Saroyan 130
Arthur Schopenhauer 46
Charles M. Schwab 20
Albert Schweitzer 17
Seneca 62, 91, 144
Shakespeare 103
Igor Sikorsky 143
Alan Simpson 52, 53
B. F. Skinner 43, 71
Socrates 103
Sophocles 145
Muriel Spark 18
Herbert Spencer 58
Adlai E. Stevenson 39
Annie Sullivan 18, 119, 136

Rabbi Tarfon 104
Allen Tate 68
Harold Taylor 69, 99
Margaret Thatcher 105
Henry David Thoreau 82
Alvin Toffler 150
Jean Toomer 86
Harry S. Truman 146
Mark Twain 27, 150
John Updike 69
Mark Van Doren 84
Vauvenargues 20
William A. Ward 132
Daniel Webster 48, 120
H. G. Wells 59
Samuel Whitbread 56
Barbara M. White 41
E. B. White 111
Alfred North Whitehead 61, 100
Ella Wheeler Wilcox 129
Eugene S. Wilson 62
Mary J. Wilson 22
John Wolfenden 69
Sydney Wood 52
William Wordsworth 149

About the Author

Criswell Freeman is a Doctor of Clinical Psychology living in Nashville, Tennessee. He is the author of *When Life Throws You a Curveball, Hit It* and numerous books in the Wisdom Series published by WALNUT GROVE PRESS.

Dr. Freeman's Wisdom Books chronicle memorable quotations in an easy-to-read style. The series provides inspiring, thoughtful and humorous messages from entertainers, athletes, scientists, politicians, clerics, writers and renegades, with each title focusing on a particular region or area of special interest. Combining his passion for quotations with extensive training in psychology, Freeman revisits timeless themes such as perseverance, courage, love, forgiveness and faith.

Dr. Freeman is also the host of *Wisdom Made in America*, a nationally syndicated radio program.

The Wisdom Series
by Dr. Criswell Freeman

Regional Titles

Wisdom Made in America	ISBN 1-887655-07-7
The Book of Southern Wisdom	ISBN 0-9640955-3-X
The Wisdom of the Midwest	ISBN 1-887655-17-4
The Wisdom of the West	ISBN 1-887655-31-X
The Book of Texas Wisdom	ISBN 0-9640955-8-0
The Book of Florida Wisdom	ISBN 0-9640955-9-9
The Book of California Wisdom	ISBN 1-887655-14-X
The Book of New York Wisdom	ISBN 1-887655-16-6
The Book of New England Wisdom	ISBN 1-887655-15-8

Sports Titles

The Golfer's Book of Wisdom	ISBN 0-9640955-6-4
The Putter Principle	ISBN 1-887655-39-5
The Golfer's Guide to Life	ISBN 1-887655-38-7
The Wisdom of Women's Golf	ISBN 1-887655-82-4
The Book of Football Wisdom	ISBN 1-887655-18-2
The Wisdom of Southern Football	ISBN 0-9640955-7-2
The Book of Stock Car Wisdom	ISBN 1-887655-12-3
The Wisdom of Old-Time Baseball	ISBN 1-887655-08-5
The Book of Basketball Wisdom	ISBN 1-887655-32-8
The Fisherman's Guide to Life	ISBN 1-887655-30-1
The Tennis Lover's Guide to Life	ISBN 1-887655-36-0

Special People Titles

Mothers Are Forever	ISBN 1-887655-76-X
Fathers Are Forever	ISBN 1-887655-77-8
Friends Are Forever	ISBN 1-887655-78-6
The Teachers' Book of Wisdom	ISBN 1-887655-80-8
The Graduates' Book of Wisdom	ISBN 1-887655-81-6
The Guide to Better Birthdays	ISBN 1-887655-35-2
Get Well Soon…If Not Sooner	ISBN 1-887655-79-4
The Wisdom of the Heart	ISBN 1-887655-34-4

Special Interest Titles

The Book of Country Music Wisdom	ISBN 0-9640955-1-3
Old-Time Country Wisdom	ISBN 1-887655-26-3
The Wisdom of Old-Time Television	ISBN 1-887655-64-6
The Book of Cowboy Wisdom	ISBN 1-887655-41-7
The Gardener's Guide to Life	ISBN 1-887655-40-9
The Salesman's Book of Wisdom	ISBN 1-887655-83-2
Minutes from the Great Women's Coffee Club (by Angela Beasley)	ISBN 1-887655-33-6

Wisdom Books are available at fine stores everywhere.
For information about a retailer near you, call 1-800-256-8584.